Congressional
Research Service
Informing the legislative debate since 1914 _____

International Monetary Fund:
Background and Issues for Congress

Martin A. Weiss
Specialist in International Trade and Finance

July 17, 2014

Congressional Research Service

7-5700

www.crs.gov

R42019

Summary

The International Monetary Fund (IMF), conceived at the Bretton Woods conference in July 1944, is the multilateral organization focused on the international monetary system. Created in 1946 with 46 members, it has grown to include 188 countries. The IMF has six purposes that are outlined in Article I of the IMF Articles of Agreement: promoting international monetary cooperation; expanding the balanced growth of international trade; facilitating exchange rate stability; eliminating restrictions on the international flow of capital; ensuring confidence by making the general resources of the Fund temporarily available to members; and adjusting balance-of-payments imbalances in an orderly manner.

Congressional interest in IMF activities has increased since the onset of the financial crisis in 2008. IMF lending has surged in recent years, particularly in light of large recent loans to Greece, Ireland, and Portugal. In 2009, major economies agreed to substantially increase the IMF's resources and to move forward on several major reforms at the institution. These include increasing the voting share of emerging economies; revamping the IMF's lending toolkit to introduce greater flexibility and create new facilities for low-income countries; and creating a road map for resolving the fast-growing economic imbalances in the global economy between surplus and deficit countries. In late 2010, IMF members agreed to a doubling of IMF quotas, which would require congressional authorization and appropriations.

The United States was instrumental in creating the IMF and is its largest financial contributor. Since voting shares are based on financial contributions, the large U.S. voting share provides the United States veto power over major decisions at the IMF. Both the IMF and its sister organization, the World Bank, are headquartered in Washington, DC.

At the Bretton Woods conference, the IMF was tasked with coordinating the system of fixed exchange rates to help the international economy recover from two world wars and the instability in the interwar period caused by competitive devaluations and protectionist trade policies. From 1946 until 1973, the IMF managed the "par value adjustable peg" system. The U.S. dollar was fixed to gold at $35 per ounce, and all other member countries' currencies were fixed to the dollar at different rates. This system of fixed rates ended in 1973 when the United States removed itself from the gold standard.

The IMF has evolved significantly as an institution since it was created. Floating exchange rates and more open capital markets in the 1990s created a new role for the IMF—the resolution of frequent and volatile international financial crises. The Asian financial crisis of 1997-1998 and subsequent crises in Russia and Latin America revealed many weaknesses of the world monetary system, which have only become more apparent in the wake of the 2008-2009 global financial crisis and the more recent sovereign debt crises in Europe.

This report evaluates the purpose, membership, financing, and focus of the IMF's activities. It also discusses the role of Congress in shaping U.S. policy at the IMF and concludes by addressing key issues, both legislative and oversight-related, that Congress may wish to consider.

Contents

Figures

Tables

Appendixes

Contacts

Introduction

This report provides background information and potential policy issues for Congress concerning the International Monetary Fund (IMF, the Fund), which is the central multilateral organization for international monetary cooperation. The United States is the largest financial contributor to the IMF. Congressional interest in IMF activities has increased since the onset of the financial crisis in 2008. IMF lending has surged in recent years, including large loans to Greece, Ireland, and Portugal. Potential policy issues for Congress include the role of the IMF as a lender of last resort, the adequacy of IMF resources, and the effectiveness of IMF surveillance of financial and monetary conditions in its member countries and of the world economy.

Background

Origins

Prior to World War II, there was no negotiated international regime governing international monetary and trade relations. It was the shared view among the allied powers that many characteristics of the international financial system during the period between the first and second world wars, including competitive devaluations, unstable exchange rates, and protectionist trade policies, worsened the 1930s depression and accelerated the onset of the war. To address these concerns, representatives of the 44 allied nations gathered in Bretton Woods, NH, in July 1944 for the United Nations Monetary and Financial Conference. Their goal was ambitious and largely successful—to create a cooperative and institutional framework for the global economy that would facilitate international trade and balanced global economic stability and growth.

At the Bretton Woods conference, Articles of Agreement for the IMF and the International Bank for Reconstruction and Development (IBRD), later known as the World Bank, were drafted and adopted. They entered into force, formally creating the institutions, on December 27, 1945, following the adoption of implementing or authorizing legislation within member countries.[1] The Articles of Agreement of both institutions constitute an international treaty, imposing obligations on member states, which have changed over time.

In the eyes of its founders, the IMF's purpose and contribution to postwar macroeconomic stability were threefold: (1) facilitate trade by restricting certain foreign exchange controls; (2) create monetary stability by managing a fixed (but flexible) exchange rate system; and (3) provide short-term financing to member countries to correct temporary balance-of-payments problems.

The U.S. Senate agreed to the ratification (by the President) of the Fund and Bank Agreements in July 1945. U.S. participation in both organizations is authorized by the United States Bretton Woods Agreement Act, as amended (Bretton Woods Act).[2] Unique among the founding members,

---

[1] The third pillar of the postwar economic agenda, negotiation on multilateral rules to liberalize and govern international trade, was not completed until the 1947 General Agreement on Tariffs and Trade (GATT). In 1995, the GATT was succeeded by the World Trade Organization (WTO).

[2] P.L. 79-171, 22 U.S.C. 286 et. seq.

the United States, in the Bretton Woods Act, requires specific congressional authorization to change the U.S. quota or "shares" in the Fund or for the United States to vote to amend the Articles of Agreement of the IMF or the World Bank. The U.S. Congress, thus, has veto power over major decisions at both institutions.

The Bretton Woods Monetary System

From 1946 to 1971, the main purpose of the IMF was regulatory, ensuring IMF members' compliance with a par value exchange rate system. This was a two-tiered currency regime using gold and the U.S. dollar. Each IMF member government could choose to define the value of its currency in terms of gold or the U.S. dollar, which the U.S. government agreed to support at a fixed gold value of one ounce of gold being equal to $35. Unlike in the classic gold standard period (1880-1914), monetary policy was not strictly restricted by a country's holdings of gold. Member countries were allowed to intervene in the currency market but were obligated to keep their exchange rates within a 1% band around their declared par value.

When currencies (other than the U.S. dollar) came under pressure from short-term "balance of payments" imbalances that normally arose through international trade and finance exchanges, countries would receive short-term financial support from the IMF. In cases where the currency "peg" was considered fundamentally misaligned, a country could devalue (or revalue) its currency. By providing monetary independence limited by the peg, the Bretton Woods monetary system combined exchange rate stability, the key benefit of the 19th century gold standard, with some of the virtues of floating exchange rates, principally independence to pursue domestic economic policies geared toward full employment.[3]

Balance-of-Payments Basics

The balance of payments is an accounting of a country's international transactions with individuals, businesses, and government agencies in that country and those in the rest of the world. It represents the sum of purely financial transactions (capital account) and those arising from the export and import of goods and services (current account), and other unilateral transfers (such as gifts or remittances).

A country's current account should be equal to the sum of the capital account and any unilateral transfers. If a country spends more abroad on goods and services than it receives, it incurs a current account deficit. The shortfall, or deficit, can be financed by selling assets or borrowing, which involves a private capital inflow into the deficit country (a capital account surplus). If, however, private sources do not cover the current account deficit, then it must be financed by the government through the sale of foreign exchange (official reserves), which is referred to as a balance-of-payments deficit.

With flexible exchange rates, the deficit (or surplus) is corrected by a market-driven adjustment to the exchange rate—that is, it depreciates or appreciates based on demand. No purchase or sale of official reserves by the government is necessary to operate a floating exchange regime. Under a pegged exchange rate system, however, countries cannot alter exchange rate values and so use their foreign exchange reserves to finance the balance-of-payments deficit, leaving the currency value intact. When a country does not have adequate foreign exchange reserves to finance its balance-of-payments deficit, it can petition the IMF for financial assistance.

The first major challenge to the postwar international monetary system came in the early 1960s. The postwar expansion in international trade and economic growth required an increase in international liquidity, that is, an increase in central bank holdings of the two major international

---

[3] Ibid.

reserve assets, gold and the U.S. dollar. With the economic recovery of Europe well advanced, the slow growth in gold supplies was hampering the growth of international reserve assets. As early as 1960, global foreign dollar holdings exceeded the value of U.S. gold holdings (at $35 an ounce). The system could continue to function as long as countries were willing to settle their balance of payments in U.S. dollars instead of gold.

The international community's response was to create a new international reserve currency, the Special Drawing Right (SDR). The SDR also serves as the IMF's unit of account. Initially defined as equivalent to 0.888671 grams of fine gold, the value of the SDR was switched to a basket of international currencies following the collapse of the Bretton Woods system of fixed parity exchange rates in 1973. The current basket includes the euro, the Japanese yen, the British pound sterling, and the U.S. dollar.

By 1970, a large and prolonged U.S. balance-of-payments deficit was mirrored by its counterpart, large balance-of-payments surpluses in the other major industrial countries. As a result, much of the 1960s was characterized by substantial currency instability, as liberalized capital flows brought about repeated currency crises in the supposedly "fixed" exchange rate Bretton Woods system. Amid declining confidence in the U.S. dollar, foreign central banks increasingly became reluctant holders of U.S. dollars and began exchanging their dollar reserves for U.S. gold holdings. After several years of instability, the Bretton Woods system of fixed exchange rates finally collapsed in March 1973 when the United States severed the link between the dollar and gold, allowing the value of its currency to be determined by market forces.

From 1973 to the Present

A major purpose of the IMF as originally conceived at Bretton Woods—to maintain fixed exchange rates—was, thus, at an end. Although the IMF had lost its motivating purpose, it adapted to the end of fixed exchange rates. In 1973, IMF members enacted a comprehensive rewrite of the IMF Articles. IMF members condoned the floating-rate exchange rate system that was already in place; officially ended the international monetary role of gold (although gold remains an international monetary asset); and, nominally, but unsuccessfully, made the SDR the world's "principal reserve asset." Henceforth, member countries were allowed to freely determine their currency's exchange rate, and use private capital flows to finance trade imbalances.

The IMF was also given two new mandates, which became the foundation of its role in the post-Bretton Woods international monetary system. The first was for the IMF to oversee the international monetary system to ensure its effective operation. The second was to oversee the compliance by member states with their new obligations to "collaborate with the Fund and other members to assure orderly exchange arrangements and to promote a stable system of exchange rates." Consequently, the IMF transformed itself from being an international monetary institution focused almost exclusively on issues of foreign exchange convertibility and stability to being a much broader international financial institution, assuming a broader array of responsibilities and engaging on a wide range of issues including financial and capital markets, financial regulation and reform, and sovereign debt resolution.

The IMF also increasingly relied on its lending powers, as floating exchange rates and the growth of international capital flows led to more frequent, and increasingly severe, financial crises. Over the past several decades, the IMF has been involved in the oil crisis of the 1970s; the Latin American debt crisis of the 1980s; the transition to market-oriented economies following the collapse of communism; currency crises in East Asia, South America, and Russia; and, most recently, the global response to the 2008-2009 global financial crisis and the 2010-2011 European sovereign debt crisis.

Institutional Aspects

Organizational Structure

The IMF Articles provide for a three-tiered governance structure with a Board of Governors, an Executive Board, and a Managing Director (**Figure 1**).

Figure 1. IMF Governance

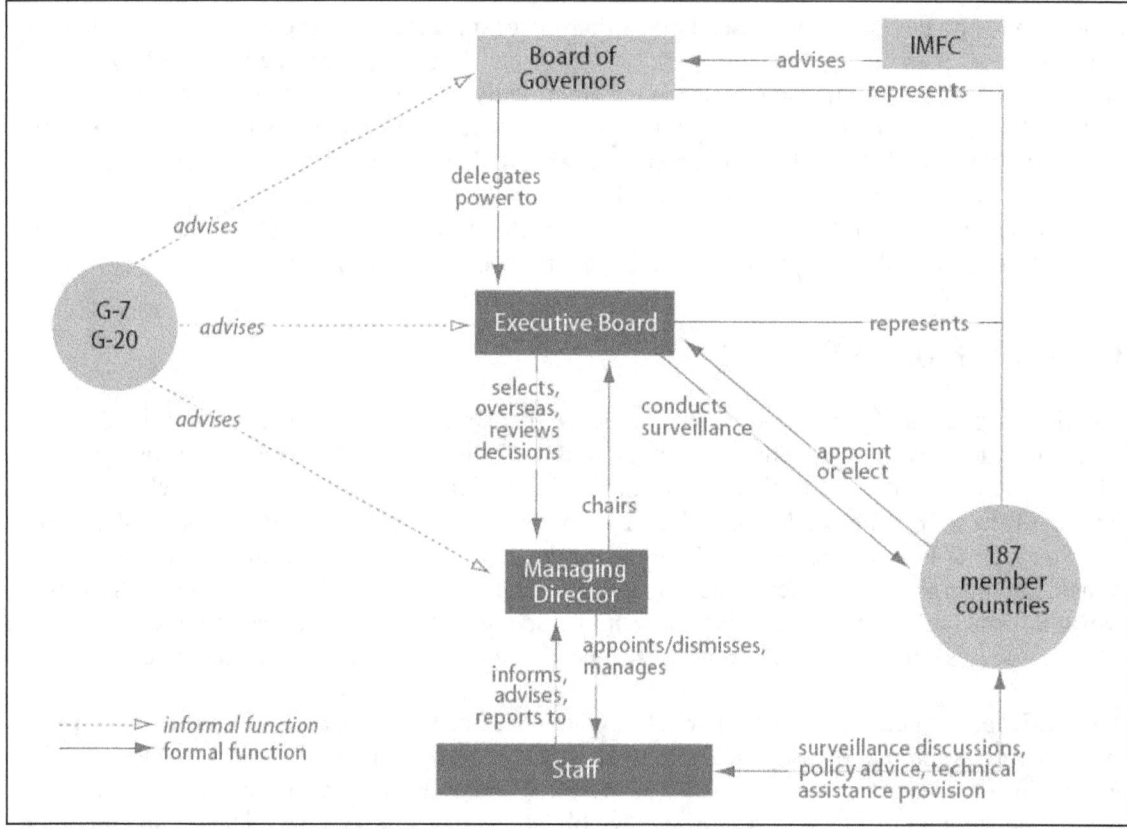

Source: International Monetary Fund, adapted by CRS.

The Board of Governors is the highest policy-making authority of the IMF. All countries are represented on the Board of Governors, usually at the finance minister or central bank governor level. IMF Governors usually meet annually at the fall IMF meetings. A committee of the Governors, the International Monetary and Financial Committee (IMFC), meets twice annually to consider major policy issues affecting the international monetary system and makes recommendations to the full Board of Governors. The Development Committee, a joint committee of the Boards of Governors of the IMF and World Bank, also meets at the same time to consider development policy issues and other matters affecting developing countries. The two committees generally issue communiqués at the close of their meetings, summarizing their findings and recommendations. These often serve as policy guidance to the IMF and the World

Bank and as a means for airing views and for coordinating or harmonizing country policies on issues of international concern.

Day-to-day authority over operational policy, lending, and other matters is vested in the Board of Executive Directors, a 24-member body that meets three or more times a week to oversee and supervise the activities of the IMF. The five largest shareholders are entitled to appoint their own Executive Director.[4] The remaining members are elected by groups of countries, generally on the basis of geographical or historical affinity. A few countries—Saudi Arabia, China, and Russia— have enough votes to elect their own Executive Directors. In reforms approved by the Governors in December 2010, the IMF Articles of Agreement will eventually be amended so that the Executive Board will consist solely of elected Directors, doing away with the practice of some member countries appointing their representatives.

The IMF Executive Board selects the Managing Director of the IMF, who serves as its chairman and chief executive officer. The Managing Director is elected for a five-year renewable term of office. The Executive Board also approves the selection of the Managing Director's principal assistants, the First Deputy Managing Director and three Deputy Managing Directors. The Managing Director manages the ongoing operations of the Fund (under the policy direction of the Executive Board); supervises some 2,800 staff members; and oversees the preparation of policy papers, loan proposals, and other documents that go before the Executive Board for its approval.

By tradition, the European countries nominate the IMF Managing Director.[5] The United States has a similar prerogative at the World Bank. The First Deputy Managing Director of the IMF is typically a U.S. citizen. Leadership selection has been a long-standing issue of concern. Emerging economic powers argue that any agreement that grants the leadership position based on nationality limits the pool of potential candidates. During the most recent transition from Dominique Strauss-Kahn to Christine Lagarde, however, non-European countries were unable to coalesce on a candidate, securing the position for a European.

Some analysts argue that calls for a non-European director from the emerging economies mask divides that make it difficult for emerging economies to unite behind one credible candidate. These calls, the argument goes, are part of the larger issue of the influence of emerging economies in the international financial institutions, and could ultimately lead to additional shifts toward emerging economies, despite Europe's hold on the top position. Evidence suggests that some shifts are underway. In July 2011, new Managing Director Lagarde elevated Zhu Min, a Chinese national serving as an advisor to the Managing Director, to Deputy Managing Director.

In addition to the official representation of the Board of Governors and the Executive Board, several other cross-cutting groups of countries are actively involved with the IMF. These include forums such as the Group of Seven (G-7) meeting of the finance ministers,[6] the Group of 20 major economies (G-20),[7] which in 2009 was declared by its members as the premier forum for

---

[4] The five largest shareholders of the IMF are the United States, Japan, Germany, France, and the United Kingdom.

[5] For more information, see CRS Report R41828, *International Monetary Fund: Selecting a Managing Director*, by Martin A. Weiss.

[6] The members of the G-7 are Canada, France, Germany, Italy, Japan, the United Kingdom, and the United States.

[7] The members of the G-20 are Argentina, Australia, Brazil, Canada, China, France, Germany, India, Indonesia, Italy, Japan, Mexico, Russia, Saudi Arabia, South Africa, Korea, Turkey, the United Kingdom, the United States, and the European Union, which is represented at the leaders' level by the presidents of the European Union and the European Commission and at the finance level by the rotating presidency of the European Council and the European Central (continued...)

international economic cooperation,[8] and the Intergovernmental Group of Twenty-Four on International Monetary Affairs and Development (G-24),[9] which coordinates the position of developing countries on monetary and development issues.

Quotas

Quotas are the primary national contribution to the IMF and are the foundation of country representation at the IMF. When a country joins the Fund, it is assigned a quota based on its relative weight in the global economy. Economic considerations include a member's GDP, openness to trade, volume of current account transactions, and level of official reserves.

A country's quota determines:

- **Subscriptions:** the amount of financial resources each member is required to contribute to the Fund;

- **Access to Financing:** the amount of financing a member may receive from the Fund; and

- **Voting Power:** the ability to formally influence the IMF's decisions.

The total of all member countries' quota subscriptions is 238 billion IMF Special Drawing Rights (SDRs), approximately $368 billion.[10] Upon joining the Fund, a country normally pays up to one-quarter of its quota, the so-called "reserve tranche," in the form of reserve assets, widely accepted foreign currencies (such as the U.S. dollar, euro, yen, pound sterling), or special drawing rights (SDRs). The remaining three-quarters are paid in the country's own currency.

Supplemental Facilities

In addition to its regular quota resources, the IMF maintains two standing multilateral borrowing arrangements—the New Arrangements to Borrow (NAB) and the General Arrangements to Borrow (GAB). These are backstop resources intended to temporarily supplement available quota resources and borrowing. If activated, participating creditor countries make loans to the IMF, and the IMF uses those funds to provide loans to eligible countries.

The NAB is a set of credit arrangements between the IMF and a group of member countries and institutions, including advanced economies and a number of emerging market countries. The NAB is the facility of first and principal recourse in circumstances in which the IMF needs to supplement its quota resources. Once activated, it can provide supplementary resources of up to SDR 367.5 billion (about $568 billion) to the IMF. The U.S. commitment to the NAB is $100

(...continued)

Bank.

[8] CRS Report R40977, *The G-20 and International Economic Cooperation: Background and Implications for Congress*, by Rebecca M. Nelson.

[9] The members of the G-24 are Algeria, Argentina, Brazil, Colombia, Côte d'Ivoire, the Democratic Republic of Congo, Egypt, Ethiopia, Gabon, Ghana, Guatemala, India, Iran, Lebanon, Mexico, Nigeria, Pakistan, Peru, Philippines, South Africa, Sri Lanka, Syria, Trinidad and Tobago, and Venezuela.

[10] International Monetary Fund, "IMF Members' Quotas and Voting Power," and "IMF Board of Governors," available at http://www.imf.org/external/np/sec/memdir/members.aspx.

---

billion.[11] The IMF does not hold the NAB funds; rather, the IMF will call on NAB members to provide a percentage of funds that these members have committed if and when the Fund needs to use them. U.S. commitments to NAB are in the possession of the United States until the IMF requests that funds be released. If NAB members choose not to activate the NAB, the GAB, which was established in 1962, allows the IMF to borrow up to $26 billion from 11 industrial countries.

Voting and Influence at the IMF

The Executive Board or Board of Governors of the IMF can approve loans, policy decisions, and many other matters by a simple majority vote. However, a supermajority vote is required to approve major IMF decisions. The supermajority may require a 70% or 85% vote, depending on the issue. A 70% majority is required to resolve financial and operational issues such as the interest rate on IMF loans or the interest rate on SDR holdings. An 85% majority is required for the most important decisions, such as the admission of new members, increases in quotas, allocations of SDRs, and amendments to the IMF's Articles of Agreement.

As **Figure 2** shows, voting at the IMF is highly concentrated, with 10 countries controlling over 50% of the voting shares (**Table 1**). With a voting share of 16.75%, the United States is the only country able to unilaterally veto major IMF decisions (i.e., those requiring an 85% majority). The United States also exercises a substantial amount of informal power at the IMF, given its large quota share and the location of the Fund in Washington, DC.[12] According to one analyst, "the IMF is an instrument of the G-7 countries. There is no example that comes easily to mind of a position taken by the IMF on any systematic issue without the tacit, if not explicit, support of the United States and the other G-7 countries."[13]

---

[11] To meet the U.S. $100 billion commitment to the expanded NAB, as well as an $8 billion increase in the U.S. quota at the IMF, Congress appropriated $5 billion in the FY2009 Spring Supplemental Appropriations for Overseas Contingency Operations (P.L. 111-32).

[12] Randall W. Stone, *Controlling Institutions: International Organizations and the Global Economy* (New York: Cambridge University Press, 2011).

[13] Lex Rieffel, *Restructuring Sovereign Debt: The Case for Ad-Hoc Machinery* (Brookings Institution Press, Washington, DC, 2003).

Figure 2. Concentration of IMF Voting Shares

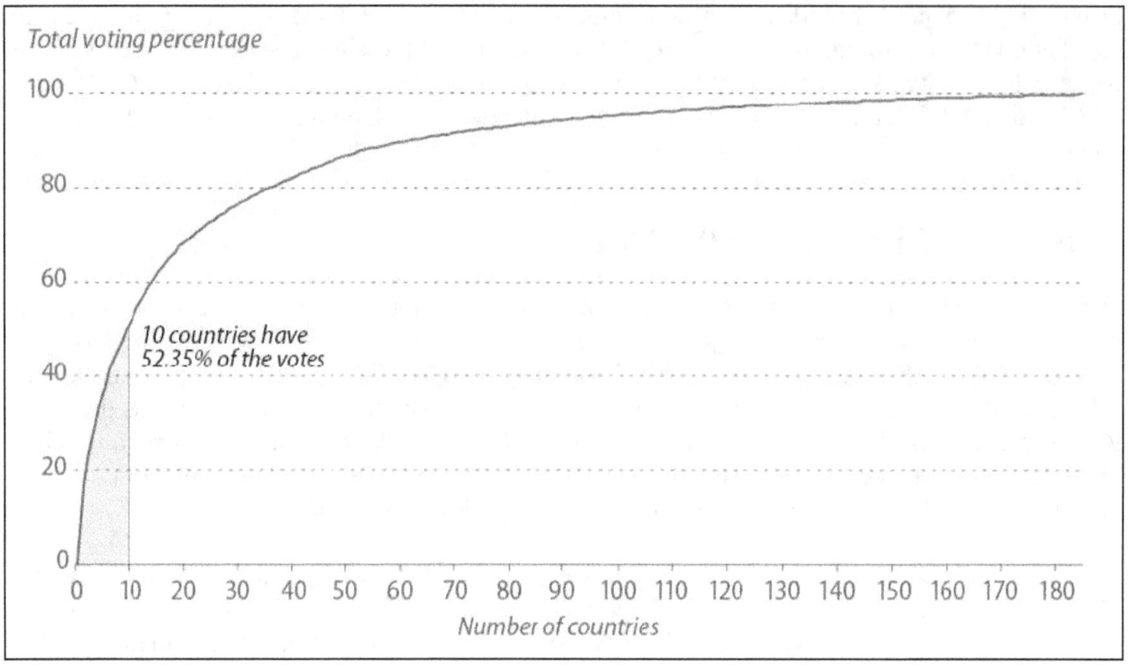

Source: International Monetary Fund.

Table 1. IMF Members with Largest Quota and Voting Shares
(as of July 10, 2014)

Member	Quota share (percentage)	Voting share (percentage)
United States	17.69	16.75
Japan	6.56	6.23
Germany	6.12	5.81
France	4.51	4.29
United Kingdom	4.51	4.29
China	4.00	3.81
Italy	3.31	3.16
Saudi Arabia	2.93	2.80
Canada	2.67	2.56
Russia	2.50	2.39

Source: International Monetary Fund.

The IMF states that its programs are based on purely economic factors, in order to seek an acceptable balance between protecting the interests of individual members and those of the membership as a whole. In practice, however, many analysts contend that the IMF is a highly politicized institution, reflecting the wide power differential between a few advanced economies and the remaining membership. For example, some analysts argue that recent IMF lending to European countries has been greater, and on more lenient terms, than lending provided to developing countries. "History suggests that if this were happening to a poor country or developing country, the rich countries would have voted against [the loan]," argues Arvind

Virmani, the Indian Executive Director at the IMF, commenting about the possibility of fresh IMF support for Greece.[14]

On account of the heavily skewed nature of IMF voting, some analysts also argue that the developing countries with strong political ties to the IMF's largest shareholders get more favorable treatment by the IMF than other developing countries. For example, researchers have found evidence that countries are more likely to receive IMF loans if their voting at the United Nations General Assembly is similar to that of the United States and other advanced economies.[15] At the same time, countries may not seek loans for the IMF, because they are politically unwilling to meet the IMF's economic conditions.

Functions of the IMF

In practice, the IMF's mandate of promoting international monetary stability translates into three main functions: (1) surveillance of financial and monetary conditions in its member countries and in the world economy; (2) financial assistance to help countries overcome major balance-of-payments problems; and (3) technical assistance and advisory services to member countries.

Surveillance

The IMF provides surveillance of the international monetary system "in order to ensure its effective operation" and to "oversee the compliance of each member with its obligations" to the Fund.[16] In particular, "the Fund shall exercise firm surveillance over the exchange rate policies of member countries and shall adopt specific principles for the guidance of all members with respect to those policies."[17] The IMF's general surveillance recommendations are not binding or enforceable. The effectiveness of IMF surveillance is dependent on the peer pressure exercised by other IMF member countries, and increasingly the global financial sector, as most IMF analysis of global economic risks is made now public.

The IMF engages in both bilateral and multilateral surveillance. IMF members agree, as a condition of membership, that they will "collaborate with the Fund and other members to assure orderly exchange arrangements and to promote a stable system of exchange rates."[18] In particular, they agree to pursue economic and financial policies that will produce orderly economic growth with reasonable price stability, to avoid erratic disruptions in the international monetary system, not to manipulate their exchange rates in order to attain unfair competitive advantage or shift economic burdens to other countries, and to follow exchange rate policies compatible with these commitments.[19]

---

[14] Alan Beattie, "IMF Warned over fresh Greek Loan," *Financial Times*, July 8, 2011.

[15] Strom Thacker, "The High Politics of IMF Lending," *World Politics*, vol. 52 (1999), pp. 38-75. See also Axel Drehar, Jan-Egbert Sturm, and James Raymond Vreeland, "Global Horse Trading: IMF Loans for Votes in the United Nations Security Council," *European Economic Review*, vol. 53 (2009), pp. 742-757.

[16] Article IV, Section 3.

[17] Ibid.

[18] Article IV, Section 1.

[19] Ibid.

Countries are required to provide the IMF with information and to consult with the IMF upon its request. The IMF staff generally meets annually with each member country for "Article IV consultations" regarding the country's current fiscal and monetary policies, the state of its economy, its exchange rate situation, and other relevant concerns. The IMF's reports on its Article IV consultations with each country are presented to the IMF Executive Board, along with the staff's observations and recommendations about possible improvements in the country's economic policies and practices.

In pursuit of its multilateral surveillance function, the IMF publishes numerous reports each year on economic conditions and trends in the world economy. These include three semiannual publications: (1) the *World Economic Outlook*, which provides analysis of the state of the global economy; (2) the *Global Financial Stability Report*, which assesses global financial markets; and (3) the *Fiscal Monitor*, which surveys and analyzes the state of public finances in member countries.

Financial Assistance

Notwithstanding its macroeconomic surveillance, the IMF is perceived as an institution that primarily provides temporary financing to troubled economies. The IMF's financial structure can best be characterized as that of a credit union (see box). IMF member countries deposit hard currency and some of their own currency, from which they can draw the currencies of other countries if they face significant problems in managing their balance of payments. As noted above, supplemental resources are available from the NAB or GAB if quota resources are insufficient.

Mechanics of IMF Financing

The IMF's financing mechanism is rooted in the credit facilities that existed between central banks prior to the IMF's creation. Central banks would borrow from each other with the borrower purchasing the currency of the lender, and paying for it by crediting the lender's account with the borrower in the borrower's currency. Thus, when borrowing from the IMF, a member purchases from the IMF the hard currency of another member in exchange for its own currency. Repayment is effected through a reversal of the original transaction. The member repays the loan by paying the IMF hard currency and repurchasing its own currency that the IMF had acquired.

For the IMF to be able to lend, it has available, through members' quota subscriptions and NAB commitments, a pool of hard currency and SDRs. A quarter of a member's quota payment is normally paid in usable assets (SDRs or currencies of other members acceptable to the IMF), and the balance is paid in the member's own currency. When members borrow from the IMF, the pool contains more of debtor members' currencies and less of SDRs or currencies of creditor members. The reverse takes place as members repay their borrowings from the IMF.

Operationally, the IMF decides quarterly, based on the expected pipeline of member borrowings and repayments, which currencies are to be used (and up to what amounts) to finance and repay its lending. The amounts transferred and received by these members are managed to ensure that their creditor positions in the IMF remain broadly even in relation to their quota, which are reported by the IMF on a quarterly basis. The most recent report, covering transactions between August 1, 2010, and October 31, 2010, reported that the U.S. creditor position was 22.5% of total quota available to finance transactions.

The IMF is required by its Articles to ensure that countries' use of its resources will be temporary and that loans will be repaid. Failure of a borrowing country to repay the IMF reduces the availability of financing for all other IMF members. In order to ensure that it gets repaid, the IMF imposes conditionality on its loans. Conditionality is also intended to correct the borrower's current account deficit by bringing about macroeconomic stabilization and economic adjustment.

In the past, there have been debates about whether the austerity conditions that are often the core of IMF conditionality are productive in increasing economic growth. In 2000, one heavily cited paper found that participating in IMF programs lowers growth rates during the program, as would be expected. In addition, however, the study found that once countries leave the program, they grow faster than if they had remained, but not faster than they would have without participating in the IMF program in the first place.[20]

After heavy criticism of the conditions attached to IMF loans to East Asia in the late 1990s, the IMF revamped its conditionality guidelines in 2002. Additional reforms, including new IMF lending instruments based on economic prequalification (ex-ante conditionality) rather than traditional structural adjustment (ex-post conditionality) also address these concerns.[21]

IMF Loan Programs

The IMF has several loan programs. The Stand-By Arrangement (SBA), which provides the bulk of IMF assistance to middle-income countries, addresses short-term balance-of-payments problems and typically lasts one to two years. The Extended Fund Facility (EFF) addresses longer-term balance-of-payments problems requiring fundamental economic reforms and generally runs for three years or longer.

In 2009, following the financial crisis, the IMF created the Flexible Credit Line (FCL). The FCL provides a credit line to countries that have strong economic fundamentals and policies, and that the credit line can be drawn on without new conditionalities being imposed. Unlike the SBA and the EFF, the FCL relies on ex-ante conditionality. As of July 2011, Colombia, Mexico, and Poland have accessed the FCL. In 2010, the IMF introduced the Precautionary Credit Line, now known as the Precautionary and Liquidity Line (PLL), for countries whose financial situations would make them ineligible for the FCL. A country can request a PLL for six months with a limit of five times its quota. The only PLL program approved to date was for Macedonia in January 2011, although many expected some Eurozone countries to request access to credit.

The IMF provides loans to its poorest member countries on concessional repayment terms. These aim to help countries overcome balance-of-payments problems, but their conditionality puts less emphasis on cutting spending and more on economic growth-enhancing reforms. There are three lending facilities for low-income countries:

- The Extended Credit Facility (ECF), which provides flexible medium-term support to low-income members that have protracted balance of payments problems.

- The Standby Credit Facility (SCF), which addresses short-term and precautionary balance of payments needs, similar to the Stand-By Arrangements in regular Fund lending.

- The Rapid Credit Facility (RCF), which provides rapid access at low levels with limited conditionality to meet urgent balance-of-payments needs.

---

[20] Adam Przeworski and James Vreeland, "The effect of IMF programs on economic growth," *Journal of Development Economics*, vol. 62 (2000).

[21] Olivier Jeanne, *Dealing with Volatile Capital Flows*, Peterson Institute for International Economics, Working Paper PB10-180, Washington, DC, July 2010.

In 2010, the Fund created the Post-Catastrophe Debt Relief (PCDR) Trust Fund to provide debt relief to low-income countries hit by catastrophic natural disasters. The first recipient of the trust was Haiti.

Finally, the Policy Support Instrument (PSI) supports low-income countries that do not want, or need, IMF lending, but seek IMF macroeconomic advice, and a "seal of approval" of their economic policies as a signal to international donors and financial markets. To date, seven countries have received support from the PSI: Cape Verde, Mozambique, Nigeria, Senegal, Uganda, Tanzania, and Rwanda.

Trends in IMF Lending

Prior to the onset of the 2008 economic crisis, many analysts argued that the IMF was on the brink of irrelevance, as booming capital flows and commodity prices allowed the remaining IMF creditors to repay their loans. With developing countries no longer needing IMF lending, and the advanced economies largely ignoring the IMF's surveillance, the Fund's future looked bleak. At the same time, IMF resources, especially when compared to global capital flows, had declined over the past few decades. Prior to the crisis, this raised little concern because demand for IMF resources was low. This view changed quickly in 2008, as the economic crisis worsened, and the IMF's loan portfolio expanded from below SDR 10 billion in 2007 to over to SDR 96.4 billion ($144.6 billion) in February 2013.[22]

Figure 3 illustrates the significant change in the composition of IMF lending since 1970. Advanced economies accounted for over 75% of the IMF credit in 1970, during the waning days of the fixed exchange rate regime. By 1990, their share of IMF credit had dropped to zero, before increasing in the late 1990s (loans to Korea and Russia), and then after the recent financial crisis. In 2010, due to several large European programs, IMF lending to advanced economies accounted for 17% of total lending. Loans to Latin America began rising in the 1970s, but did not increase sharply until the 1980s debt crises, peaking in 1990. Loans increased after 2000 because of three large programs (Argentina, Brazil, and Uruguay), but have since declined, and are now at historically low levels, along with Asian economies.

---

[22] For more information, see CRS Report RS22976, *The Global Financial Crisis: The Role of the International Monetary Fund (IMF)*, by Martin A. Weiss.

Figure 3. Outstanding IMF Credit, 1970-2010

(percentage of total outstanding credit)

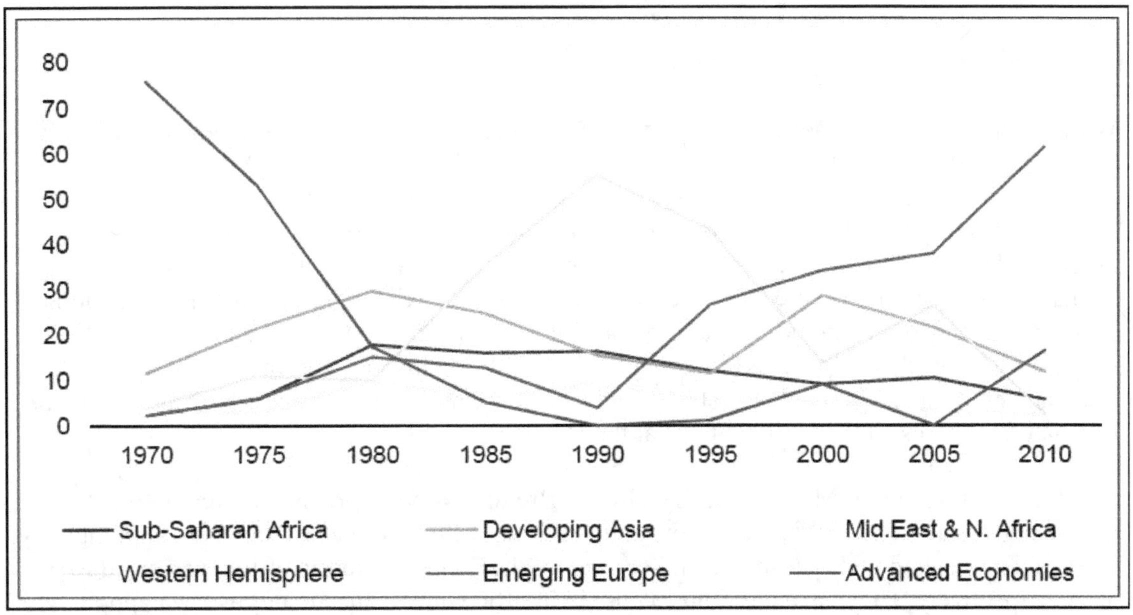

Source: International Monetary Fund.

Another key trend is the increasing size of IMF loans compared to a country's quota. Officially, the amount a country is able to borrow from the IMF is related to the country's quota, its ownership and contribution share in the IMF. In most instances, countries may borrow several multiples of their quota in response to particular circumstances. The conditionality and performance standards attached to a loan become more rigorous and demanding as its size (relative to the borrower's quota) increases. In many cases, deemed exceptional by the IMF executive board at the time, countries have received much larger loans from the IMF than are allowed under normal guidelines. The 2010 loan to Greece, for example, was 3,212% of Greece's quota at the IMF. The 2011 loan to Ireland was 2,322% of its quota.

Technical Assistance

Access to technical assistance is one benefit of IMF membership, accounting for about 20% of the IMF's annual operating budget. The IMF provides technical assistance in its core areas of expertise: macroeconomic policy; tax and revenue policies; expenditure management; exchange rates; financial sector sustainability; and economic statistics. IMF technical assistance supports the development of the productive resources of member countries by helping them to effectively manage their economic policy and financial affairs. The IMF helps these countries to strengthen their capacity in both human and institutional resources, and to design appropriate macroeconomic, financial, and structural policies. About 90% of IMF technical assistance goes to low and lower-middle income countries.[23]

---

[23] International Monetary Fund, *Fact Sheet: IMF Lending*, March 30, 2011.

U.S. Engagement with the IMF

U.S. Policy-Making Process

As the largest single shareholder of IMF quota (approximately $67.35 billion), and contributor to the NAB ($100 billion), the United States has a leading role in shaping the IMF's lending, surveillance, and advisory operations. While the statutory framework for U.S. participation in the IMF provides the President the authority to appoint the U.S. Governor, Alternate Governor, Executive Director, and Alternate Executive Director, the Department of the Treasury has been delegated responsibility to direct U.S. representatives at the IMF and to take a range of actions with respect to the IMF, including making contributions to capital increases and implementing congressional mandates. Congress is responsible for authorizing and appropriating all U.S. financial commitments to the IMF. The Senate has advise and consent authority over all persons nominated to represent the United States at the IMF.

U.S. participation in the IMF is authorized by the Bretton Woods Agreements Act of 1945.[24] U.S. representatives at the Board of Governors and the Board of Executive Directors are appointed by the President, by and with the advice and consent of the Senate, to terms of five years and two years, respectively. They have the right to remain in office until a successor has been appointed.[25] The Secretary of the Treasury, as a matter of practice, is nominated to serve as the U.S. Governor at the IMF. The Chairman of the Federal Reserve customarily is nominated to serve as the U.S. Alternate Governor. As discussed above, the Board of Governors has delegated substantial authority to the IMF's Executive Board, which carries out the IMF's day-to-day operations. The U.S. Executive Director and Alternate U.S. Executive Director serve as representatives of the United States to the IMF and present the U.S. government's positions. Executive Directors at the IMF, including those of those of the United States, are employees of the IMF.[26]

When the United States joined the IMF, Congress made an interagency group of executive branch agencies, the National Advisory Council on International Monetary and Financial Problems (NAC), responsible for instructing the U.S. IMF representative, under the general direction of the President. Unless the President overrode their recommendations, policy was determined by a majority vote of agencies involved. The initial interagency procedure did not work well, and in 1965, Congress approved a reorganization act that abolished the NAC as a statutory committee and transferred all of its responsibilities and authority to the President, including the responsibility for instructing U.S. representatives at the IMF. In 1966, President Lyndon Johnson delegated the responsibility to direct U.S. representatives at the IMF to the Treasury Department, where it continues to reside today.[27] The President reconstituted the NAC by executive order, but

---

[24] 22 U.S.C. 286 et seq.

[25] 22 U.S.C. 286a (a), (b).

[26] Federal law limits the salaries that IMF may pay the U.S. representatives, capping them at the rate of level IV of the Executive Schedule for the U.S. Executive Director and level V for the Alternate U.S. Executive Director.

[27] Executive Order 11269 of February 14, 1966, as amended, specifically delegates to the Secretary of the Treasury the President's authority to instruct representatives of the United States to the international financial organizations and to provide the U.S. government's consent with respect to IMF decisions. In addition, 22 U.S.C. 6593 specifically provides the Department of the Treasury with the primary responsibility to continue to coordinate "activities relating to United States participation in international financial institutions and relating to organization of multilateral efforts aimed at currency stabilization, currency convertibility, debt reduction, and comprehensive economic reform programs."

it became solely a forum where other agencies could advise the Treasury Department about policy concerns regarding U.S. participation in the international financial institutions.[28]

Unlike in a U.S. government department or agency, changes in the IMF's operations cannot be brought about simply by changing U.S. law. As a result, congressional proposals for policy changes in the IMF are formulated as directives to the Secretary of the Treasury to instruct the representative of the U.S. government in the IMF, the U.S. Executive Director, to promote the desired change. These have often been formulated as an instruction to use the "voice and vote" of the United States to achieve the desired goal. Consequently, the term "voice and vote" has become something of a generic or descriptive term for those amendments to U.S. law that seek to bring about specific changes within the IMF. Over the years, "voice and vote" amendments have increased. In the context of the current debate over IMF funding for advanced European economies, questions have arisen over the extent to which congressional policy, as embodied in the "voice and vote" amendments, has been carried out.

Voice and vote amendments can be organized in three broad categories: "policy," "directed vote," and "reporting." Policy mandates seek to foster or advocate certain policies at the IMF by directing the Treasury Department to instruct the U.S. Executive Director to use his or her "voice" and/or "vote" on behalf of the United States at the IMF Executive Board. For example, the U.S. Executive Director is directed to (1) encourage the IMF to adopt internationally recognized worker rights for borrowing countries; (2) encourage and promote the integration of women into the national economies of IMF member countries and into professional positions within the IMF organization; and (3) urge the IMF to encourage member countries to pursue macroeconomic stability while promoting environmental protection.

The second category, directed voting mandates, require that the U.S. Executive Director oppose an IMF loan when a country meets or does not meet certain criteria. In practice, U.S. opposition can take the form of abstaining from voting on, or voting against, the IMF loan under consideration. Examples include when a country has been determined by the President to violate religious freedom, provide support for acts of international terrorism, or engage in the proliferation of nuclear weapons.

Reporting requirements, the third category, require Treasury to report to Congress on various issues related to U.S. participation in the IMF. Congress enacted legislation in 2010, for example, that requires the Treasury Department to report regularly to Congress about economic conditions in heavily indebted advanced economies receiving IMF assistance.[29] These reports are to discuss the debt status of the borrower country, economic conditions affecting its vulnerability and its ability to repay, and its debt management status.

---

[28] Since 1999, Congress has required that Treasury, as Chairman of the NAC, annually report to Congress on several topics related to U.S. participation in the international financial institutions, including an assessment of the effectiveness of the major policies and operations of the international financial institutions; the major issues affecting United States participation; progress made and steps taken to achieve U.S. policy goals (including major policy goals embodied in current law).

[29] For more information, see CRS Report R41239, *Frequently Asked Questions about IMF Involvement in the Eurozone Debt Crisis*, coordinated by Rebecca M. Nelson, p. 22.

Authorizing and Appropriating U.S. Contributions to the IMF

As discussed above, quota increases are paid to the IMF by transferring 25% of the increase in hard currency and the remainder in national currency, typically through a letter of credit. Both hard currency payments and payments to the IMF under the quota letter of credit result in a budget expenditure only if cash is actually transferred to the IMF. When a transfer is made, however, the United States gets an equal and offsetting receipt—an interest-bearing, liquid international monetary asset, specifically the increase in the U.S. reserve position in the Fund. Under current budgetary conventions, these offsetting transactions are treated as an exchange of assets. As a consequence, they do not result in net budget outlays, and they do not affect the net budgetary position (deficit or surplus) of the federal government. Looked at another way, any debt (liability) incurred through the sale of securities to make this expenditure is balanced by an asset—the U.S. reserve position in the Fund.

Nonetheless, Members of Congress have often provided authorization and appropriations to increase the U.S. quota, reflecting congressional concern about increasing U.S. foreign liabilities, and their impact on the federal budget.

Budgetary treatment for the NAB is identical to that of IMF quota increases: an exchange of assets, having no net effect on the U.S. fiscal position. A drawing by the IMF under the NAB would not constitute a contribution to the IMF's capital and would not, therefore, increase the U.S. reserve position in the IMF. Rather, it would constitute an interest-bearing loan to the IMF. **Table 2** provides U.S. contributions since the IMF's creation, and their budgetary treatment. An **Appendix** provides additional information on the budgetary treatment of U.S. contributions to the IMF.

Table 2. Budgetary Treatment of U.S. Contributions to the IMF

Event	Date Effective	U.S. contribution (approximate billions of U.S. dollars)	Budgetary Treatment	Appropriation (Yes/No)
Founding Subscription	1945	$2.75	Outlay	No
Quota increase	1959	$1.375	Outlay	No
Establish General Agreements to Borrow (GAB)	1962	$2.00	None	Yes
Quota increase	1966	$1.035	25% outlay, remainder issued as line of credit, outlay on call only	Yes
Quota increase	1970	$1.54	No outlay, exchange of monetary assets	Yes
Quota increase	1978	$2.10	No outlay, exchange of monetary assets	No
Participate in Supplemental Finance Facility	1978	$1.87	No outlay, exchange of monetary assets	No
Quota increase	1980	$5.34	No outlay, exchange of monetary assets	Yes
Quota increase	1983	$5.58	No outlay, exchange of monetary assets	Yes
GAB increase	1983	$2.45	No outlay, exchange of monetary assets	Yes
Quota increase	1992	$11.92	No outlay, exchange of monetary assets	Yes
Quota increase	1998	$14.55	No outlay, exchange of monetary assets	Yes
Establish New Arrangements to Borrow (NAB)	1998	$3.4	No outlay, exchange of monetary assets	Yes
Ad hoc quota increase	2009	$8.00	Outlay, credit reform scoring adjusted for market risk	Yes
NAB increase	2009	$100.00	Outlay, credit reform scoring adjusted for market risk	Yes

Source: C. Randall Henning, *U.S. Interests and the International Monetary Fund*, Peterson Institute for International Economics, Policy Brief no. 09-12, Washington, DC, June 2009.

Policy Issues for Congress

Increased attention to the IMF since the financial crisis has revived long-standing debates about the institution's role in the global economy and the future of U.S. support for the institution. Some analysts argue that with the end of the pegged-exchange rate system, the IMF is no longer needed and it should be abolished.[30] Others say the IMF is still vital, but needs to be restructured and refocused.[31] Still others suggest that new functions should be added to the IMF and its role in the international monetary system should be expanded.[32]

Events since 2008 have shown that substantial risks remain in the global economy. Global imbalances, exchange rate misalignment, volatile capital flows and exchange rate movements, and the accumulation of large stockpiles of foreign exchange reserves have led many analysts to question the functioning of the international monetary system, and by extension, the future of the IMF.

Two issues that Congress may wish to consider are (1) should the IMF act as an international lender of last resort; and (2) are the resources of the IMF adequate to complete this function?

A central challenge for the global economy, according to some analysts, is the lack of an international lender of last resort that has access to sufficient finance to prevent a systemic global financial crisis.[33] Cross-border financial integration has brought many benefits, through trade and increased access to financing, but has also increased the risk of contagion, whereby a crisis may spread beyond its borders to other, seemingly stable economies. This is especially evident among advanced economies, where many analysts argue that the proliferation of credit in the financial system—among advanced economies, gross assets and liabilities are 500% of GDP—reflects significant economic distortions in the underlying economies. As the recent 2008 financial crisis illustrated, a single event, the bankruptcy of Lehman Brothers, can trigger a sharp contraction of global capital flows in such a highly connected global economy (**Figure 4**).

---

[30] Amar Bhide and Edmund Phelps, "More Harm Than Good: How the IMF's Business Model Sabotages Properly Functioning Capitalism," *Newsweek*, July 11, 2011.

[31] Edwin Truman, *On What Terms is the IMF Worth Funding?*, Peterson Institute for International Economics, WP 08-11, Washington, DC, December 2008.

[32] Barry Eichengreen, *Out-of-the-Box Thoughts on the International Financial System*, International Monetary Fund, Working Paper no. 09-116, Washington, DC, May 2009.

[33] In a national economy, this function is typically provided by the central bank. See CRS Report RS21986, *Federal Reserve: Lender of Last Resort Functions*, by Marc Labonte.

Figure 4. Increasing Global Linkages and Risks

(percent of GDP, unless otherwise indicated)

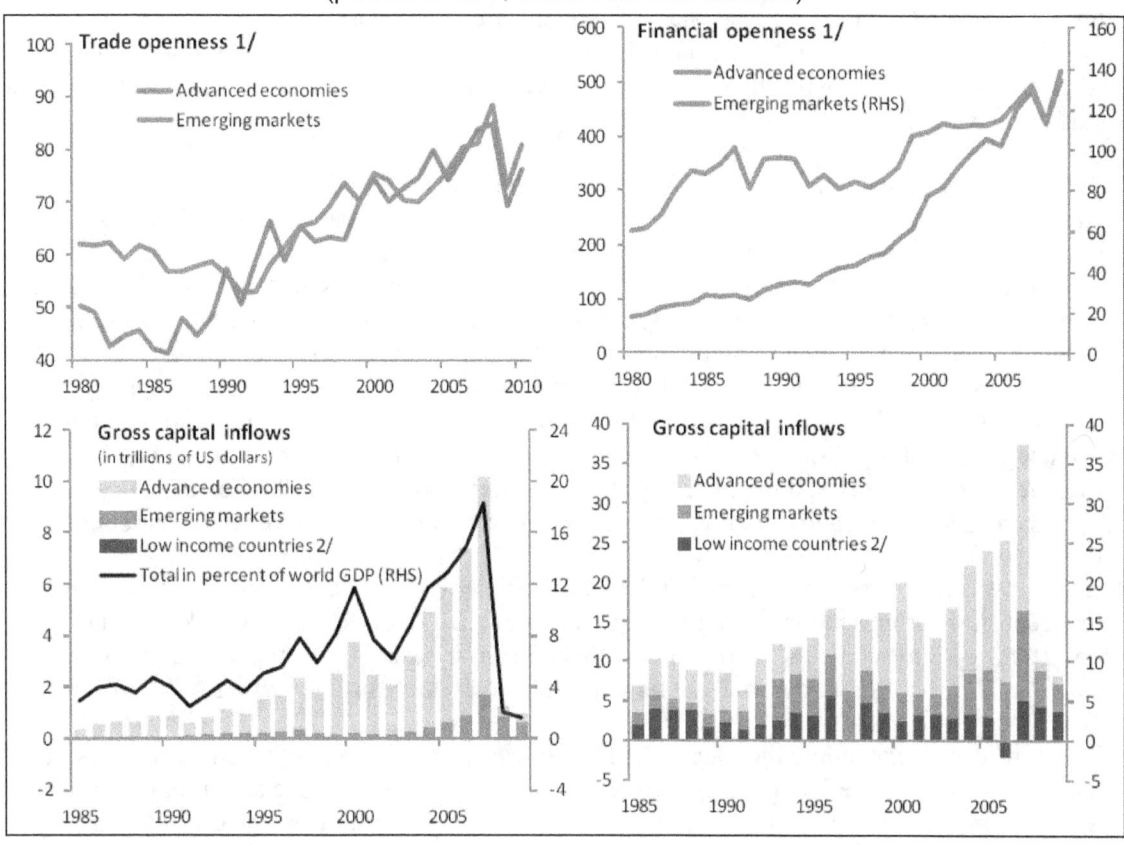

Source: International Monetary Fund.

Notes: (1) Trade openness is the sum of exports and imports as a share of GDP. Financial openness is the sum of external assets and liabilities as a share of GDP. (2) As classified in the IMF *World Economic Outlook*.

The challenge facing the international monetary system, and thus the IMF, is described by economist Maurice Obstfeld:

> In a world of integrated financial centers and multiple currencies, the boundaries within which a central bank can function as a last-resort lender no longer correspond to the boundaries within which a liquidity shortage *in its currency* can arise. Furthermore, the globally interdependent nature of modern financial relationships ensures that market turmoil *outside* the central bank's jurisdiction may well migrate *inside*. This is the basic problem.[34]

While many emerging and some advanced economies drew on IMF resources during the recent financial crisis, the majority resorted to an ad hoc network of central bank swap arrangements. At the height of the crisis, in the face of a massive global shortage of dollars, the U.S. Federal Reserve deployed over $600 billion in global liquidity to many other advanced and emerging economies, double the available resources of the IMF. The European Central Bank (ECB) set up €250 ($360) billion in swap lines, of which about €200 ($288) billion was with the U.S. Fed. In

---

[34] Maurice Obstfeld, *Expanding Gross Asset Positions in the International Monetary System*, remarks at the Federal Reserve Bank of Kansas City symposium on "Macroeconomic Challenges: The Decade Ahead," Jackson Hole, Wyoming, August 26-28, 2010.

October 2008, the Fed also authorized swap lines of $30 billion each to four emerging economies with large exposure to U.S. financial institutions, Brazil, South Korea, Mexico, and Singapore. Thus, the Fed, and not the IMF, was the de facto lender of last resort for major economies. At the same time, several other countries, primarily in Asia, relied on their accumulation of foreign exchange reserves built up during the 2000s to prevent their economies from collapsing due to the liquidity crisis.

While central bank swap lines and self-insurance through reserve accumulation were effective in mitigating the effects of the crisis, and restoring liquidity in the global economy, the costs associated with these mechanisms are substantial, both for individual countries and for the system as a whole.[35] By their very nature, the Fed and ECB swap lines were selective, and subject to domestic monetary policy, as well as political pressure. It is uncertain whether the United States will be willing to play this role again in the future. Large accumulation of foreign exchange reserves is expensive, since they typically earn little interest and are susceptible to exchange rate risk. They also contribute to systemic instability, by creating excessive demand for reserve currencies, thus putting downward pressure on interest rates in the economies of reserve currencies, such as the U.S. dollar. Large swings in official portfolios of foreign exchange reserves can also have significant impact on exchange rates and the price of sovereign bonds.

Some analysts have proposed improving the Fund's lender of last resort function. For example, one recent study proposed three main elements of what such reform could look like: (1) an automatic trigger to access the facility; (2) unilateral country prequalification to the facility during Article IV consultations; and (3) liquidity funded by the world's "issuers of last resort."[36]

When considering expanding the role of the IMF, however, the concept of moral hazard has often been considered. As IMF lending increased after the financial crisis, especially after the large loans to Greece, Ireland, and Portugal, many observers, including some Members of Congress, raised concerns that financing by the IMF, particularly emergency financing provided during financial crises, encouraged the very behavior that it sought to prevent. Simply put, IMF lending may send the wrong signals to government officials. According to this view, in the best-case scenario, countries are spared the worst consequences of their poor economic decisions. In other cases, the IMF program may not stabilize the crisis, further indebting the crisis-afflicted country.

Other analysts argue that, as the 1994-1995 Mexican crisis, the 1997-1999 Asian crisis, and the recent 2008 crisis have demonstrated, residents of IMF-recipient countries suffer painful consequences of a forced economic adjustment. The policy question is whether economic pain is mitigated by external financial support tied to a conditional economic adjustment program. A different type of "moral hazard" also arises with regard to investors. Does the existence of an emergency financial mechanism encourage private investors to take on risks that they might otherwise shun in an attempt to reap greater financial returns? In this context, some are troubled that, as a by-product of a "bailout," professional investors, who took on higher risks and were probably rewarded with higher returns, are made whole.

---

[35] Maurice Obstfeld, Jay C. Shambaugh, and Alan M. Taylor, *Financial Instability, Reserves, and Central Bank Swap Lines in the Panic of 2008*, National Bureau of Economic Research, NBER Working Paper No. 14826, March 2009.

[36] Eduardo Fernandez-Arias and Eduardo Levy Yeyati, *Global Financial Safety Nets: Where Do We Go from Here?*, Inter-American Development Bank, IDB Working Paper 231, November 2010.

IMF conditionality and pre-qualification of IMF loans might reduce concerns about moral hazard. Edwin Truman at the Peterson Institute for International Economics argues that the IMF's role can be improved, addressing moral hazard at the same time, through a "comprehensive prequalification" process where the Fund presents "policy terms for lending" to every member country potentially eligible to borrow from the IMF, based on the IMF's bilateral and multilateral economic surveillance.[37]

Adequacy of IMF Resources

To address the increased demand for IMF resources, world leaders at the spring 2009 G-20 meeting in London agreed to substantially boost the IMF's lending capacity, primarily by a $500 billion increase in the size of the NAB. The Obama Administration proposed that the United States contribute up to $100 billion.[38] The requisite authorizations and appropriations were included in the FY2009 Spring Supplemental Appropriations for Overseas Contingency Operations (P.L. 111-32).

One of the reasons that world leaders increased IMF resources in 2009 via the NAB, and not through an increase in quotas, was long-standing frustration among emerging market economies that, after years of sustained economic growth, their representation at the IMF did not reflect their current economic position in the world economy.[39] Simply put, many emerging economies were unwilling to increase the IMF's quota resources, unless there was also a shift in their share of IMF quota relative to the advanced economies that had traditionally dominated the institution. At the same time, a broad consensus has emerged that some European countries are over-represented at the IMF compared to their share of global GDP, especially in light of their representation on the Executive Board. European countries have three full seats on the IMF Executive Board, and currently chair or co-chair seven of the group constituencies.

At the April 2010 G-20 meetings, leaders pledged a shift of at least 5% of the IMF quota share to under-represented countries. On November 11-12, 2010, IMF member states agreed on a package of reforms, the core of which is a doubling of overall IMF quota to about $755 billion. In addition, there would be a significant shift of voting power to dynamic emerging market economies. If the reforms are implemented, the 10 largest members of the IMF will consist of the United States; Japan; the four largest European economies (France, Germany, Italy, and the United Kingdom); and Brazil, China, India, and Russia.

The quota increase is expected to come via a repositioning of the NAB resources that were pledged in 2009. As part of the new quota increase to be completed by September 2012, member countries' commitments to the NAB are expected to be proportionally reduced to fund the increase in their quota.

Action by Congress will likely be required for the United States to participate in this plan.[40] According to one analyst, for the United States to participate in the quota increase, Congress

---

[37] Edwin Truman, *The IMF as International Lender of Last Resort*, Peterson Institute for International Economics, Real Time Economic Issues Watch, October 12, 2010.

[38] CRS Report R40578, *The Global Financial Crisis: Increasing IMF Resources and the Role of Congress*, by Jonathan E. Sanford and Martin A. Weiss.

[39] CRS Report RL33626, *International Monetary Fund: Reforming Country Representation*, by Martin A. Weiss.

[40] For more information, see CRS Report R42844, *IMF Reforms: Issues for Congress*, by Rebecca M. Nelson and (continued...)

would need to authorize a shift of about $65 billion from the funds appropriated for increased U.S. IMF participation in the FY2009 Supplemental Appropriations Act.[41] In addition to increasing the size and composition of IMF quota, there was also agreement on some governance reform of the IMF Executive Board, which would also need congressional approval since the IMF's Articles must be amended for them to take effect. These include

- the transfer of two European chairs to emerging market countries;

- the move to an all-elected Executive Board, eliminating the practice of appointing Executive Directors and allowing all countries to participate in Executive Director elections;[42] and

- establishment of a second alternate Executive Director position for multi-country constituencies with at least seven countries.[43]

The quota and governance reforms are interlinked, and cannot be implemented separately. A double majority of the IMF membership (voting power and number of total members) is required to adopt the reforms. For the quota increase, IMF members representing at least 70% of IMF contributions must consent to the increase. The governance reforms must be agreed by three-fifths of the IMF's 188 members (113 members) having 85% of the IMF's total voting power. In many cases (including the United States) this involves parliamentary approval. Since the United States has voting power of 16.75%, the reforms cannot become effective without ratification by the United States.

(...continued)

Martin A. Weiss.

[41] Edwin Truman, IMF Governance Reform: A "Pretty Good" Step in the Right Direction, *Peterson Institute for International Economics*, November 8, 2010.

[42] Currently, members holding the five largest voting positions at the Fund appoint an Executive Director and are unable to participate in the elections that decide nominated Executive Directors.

[43] International Monetary Fund, "Factsheet: IMF Quotas," March 3, 2011.

Appendix. U.S. Contributions to the IMF and the Federal Budget

When the United States joined the IMF, and for the first two quota increases, U.S. contributions were appropriated and recorded as an outlay on the federal budget. In 1967, the President's Commission on Budget Concepts recommended that U.S. transfers to the IMF be reflected on the federal budget as an exchange of monetary assets of equivalent value to the United States from the IMF, and therefore that they not be recorded in the federal budget as an outlay.

At the time of the next IMF quota increase, which became effective on October 30, 1970, the new budgetary concepts applicable to U.S. transactions with the IMF were not fully implemented. As a result, the transaction was treated as an exchange of assets rather than as an outlay in the official budget, as recommended by the President's Commission on Budget Concepts. For the next quota increase, which became effective in 1978, the U.S. share was subject to the budgetary treatment recommended by the commission: the quota increase was an exchange of monetary assets involving no budgetary outlay and requiring no appropriation.

At the time of congressional debate on the 1980 quota increase, Congress and the Administration agreed to incorporate appropriations legislation to reflect the fact that U.S. commitment to the IMF represented a line of credit. As such, Congress wanted control over the amount of contingent liability the United States undertook through its participation in the IMF. Since the United States received an equal asset at the IMF, and nobody could predict whether there would be any eventual outlays, a compromise was reached whereby U.S. contributions to the IMF (either quota or NAB) would score as budget authority (an act of appropriations would be required), but the contributions would continue to be scored as zero (i.e., no cost) on the federal budget, thus incurring no budget outlays (no effect on deficits/surplus).

In spring 2009, President Obama requested an increase in U.S. contributions to the IMF. When the request was transmitted to Congress, President Obama argued that treatment for U.S. contributions to the IMF should revert to the pre-1980 standard, and thus neither require budget authority nor incur any outlays. While many agreed with the Administration that it was unusual to record budget authority and not outlays, some Members of Congress raised concerns about not scoring any outlays for additional U.S. contributions to the IMF. They argued that such a method did not correctly reflect the degree of risk of the IMF defaulting on the U.S. contribution, given the current economic turmoil.

After several months of negotiation, on May 12, 2009, the White House and Congress reached an agreement to treat the U.S. subscription to the IMF as a line of credit for budgetary purposes. The Federal Credit Reform Act of 1990 provides that when the U.S. government makes a loan, it does not need to include the full face value of the loan in the federal budget. Rather, Congress must appropriate the estimated subsidy cost, an amount equal to the amount the U.S. government might lose from these loans as a consequence of defaults.[44] This procedure is used throughout the federal budgeting process. Unlike IMF quota increases since 1967, the U.S. contribution would be scored as a loan for budgetary purposes under the existing credit reform legislation with a

---

[44] See out-of-print CRS Report RL30346, *Federal Credit Reform: Implementation of the Changed Budgetary Treatment of Direct Loans and Loan Guarantees*, by James M. Bickley (available upon request).

commensurate budgetary impact. In the law authorizing U.S. participation in the new IMF funding plans, the FY2009 Spring Supplemental Appropriations for Overseas Contingency Operations, Congress subsequently appropriated $5 billion as a loan loss reserve to cover the risk associated with the new U.S. payments to the IMF.[45]

Author Contact Information

Martin A. Weiss
Specialist in International Trade and Finance
mweiss@crs.loc.gov, 7-5407

Acknowledgments

Amber Wilhelm provided graphics support on this report.

---

[45] CRS Report R40531, *FY2009 Spring Supplemental Appropriations for Overseas Contingency Operations*, coordinated by Stephen Daggett and Susan B. Epstein.